George Carey's

The Church in the Market Place

Study Guide

Michael P. Knowles

MOREHOUSE PUBLISHING
Harrisburg, PA

Morehouse Publishing
P.O. Box 1321
Harrisburg, PA 17105

ISBN: 0-8192-1607-0 Study Guide

Printed in the United States of America
by
BSC LITHO
Harrisburg, PA 17105

Preface

In his "Preface to the Second Edition," Carey makes four suggestions as to how his book might be used by other congregations:

a) "First, please note that the central emphasis falls on spiritual renewal . . . let your controlling principle be Christ and his will your delight."

b) "Second, if change in any form is planned, set mission and outreach before you as your primary goals."

c) "Third, try to be proactive rather than reactive."

d) "Fourthly, the story of *The Church in the Market Place* is the story of ordinary people finding that God's power is available and his grace is all-sufficient."

As you begin to read and study *The Church in the Market Place*, which of these seems most important for your congregation right now, which have you already put into practice, and which comes next?

HOW TO USE THIS STUDY GUIDE

The following questions will help to guide your reflection on this book, either individually or as a member of a study group. In a study group, remember to allow time at the beginning for group members to discuss the content of the chapter or chapters you want to focus on. Then discuss the questions in the Study Guide, allowing each member of the group the opportunity to contribute. If you discover that you do not have time for all of the questions, or that some questions seem more relevant than others, feel free to skip the questions that do not apply to your situation.

In a congregational setting, study of *The Church in the Market Place* can be combined with a series of presentations from church leaders who discuss the process of spiritual renewal at work in their own congregations. Encourage the speakers to compare their own experiences to the situation Carey describes, so as to provide a starting point for your discussion. Each of the questions provided on the following pages can then be applied to the congregation that the speaker has discussed, to your own congregation, or to both (whichever is most helpful).

Chapter 1

Renewal

In Chapter One, "Renewal," Carey describes his own transformation from being a Christian with a "spiritual void" inside to having "a great love of Christ, a deep desire to read the Scriptures, a longing to share the Christian faith with others and a desire to praise God." The change came about when, deeply troubled by his own lack of spiritual vitality, he prayed to God, "Unless you fill me again with your Spirit, I cannot go on!"

Where on the following scale would you place yourself and/or your congregation:

Christian Spiritual Void ____________

Praying for God's Spirit ____________

"A great love of Christ" ____________

Chapter 2

Your Church Is On Fire!

Chapter Two, "Your Church is on Fire!," contains the following quotes:

- "Unless the church is prepared to meet regularly in fellowship and to grow closer together, it will not fulfill its mission as a church."
- "Renewal begins with prayer."
- "Another great concern was worship."
- "The problem was one of mission."
- "I gradually learned that cleaning up such foul abuse of a place I loved could be a lowly symbol of my relationship to Christ."
- "Opening the church in that way revealed the [physical] deficiencies of St Nic's as a place of fellowship."
- "The real significance lay in the fact that we had begun to give *sacrificially*."

Decide which of these are the three top priorities for your congregation: is there one particular ministry or area of concern that you would like to take on?

__ Midweek Fellowship	__ Serving
__ Prayer	__ Physical facilities
__ Worship	__ Sacrificial giving
__ Mission	

Chapter 3

You Have Destroyed My Church

Chapter Three, "You Have Destroyed My Church," describes some of the conflict that changes in worship produced among members of the congregation. Carey notes that these changes were motivated by the desire both to "meet a real need in the congregation" and to draw newcomers to God. Since the changes were undergirded by "a quiet conviction that we were following God's will," he concludes that the conflict arose out of a difference in people's vision for the church.

What have been the motives for change in your congregation, in what ways has conflict resulted, and what (if anything) has brought resolution? In light of your congregation's experience, what do you make of Carey's statement that "faith—to be true faith—always contains an element of risk"?

Chapter 4

Song and Dance

Chapter Four, "Song and Dance," contains David Watson's advice on the spiritual renewal of a congregation:

> **"Clarify the vision. Make sure that what you want to achieve are God's objectives and not your own fancies. A Spirit-filled church is not built overnight. It comes as a result of a spiritual, praying congregation who are prepared to go all the way with God."**

Five essential elements here are prayer, clarity of vision, submission to God's purposes, commitment, and willingness to persevere. At what stage are you and your congregation right now:

__ Praying
__ Clarifying the vision
__ Making sure of God's objectives
__ Preparing to "go all the way with God"
__ Persevering in building a "Spirit-filled church"

Chapter 5

Build My Church

Chapter Five, "Build My Church," describes a process of change that began with the question, "Is there anything attractive about us that might draw others in?" In answering that question, St Nic's congregation was guided by their recognition of urgent needs in the surrounding community, the conviction that "if this is God's will for the church, then we must assume that he will provide and equip us," and a series of "God's coincidences" which proved this assumption to be true.

In your own church, what is the most attractive feature that could draw others in, and which area of guidance is most important for you right now: recognition of needs, stronger faith in God's plan, or the actual experience of God's provision?

Chapter 6

Renew My People

In Chapter Six, "Renew My People," a discouraging reversal leads to deeper insight into God's priorities for spiritual renewal. After months of prayer and careful deliberation by the congregation, St Nic's Church Council rejects a proposed plan to renovate the church building. But in the midst of their disappointment, they hear God saying, "I am more interested in you than a fine building. Unless you are renewed, a lovely place is beside the point. When you are made alive then I will bring this thing to pass."

Have you or your congregation experienced similar reversals in your spiritual growth and, if so, what insights were you able to gain? As a result, what do you think God is saying about his priorities for spiritual renewal in your church?

Chapter 7

The Spirit Moves

Chapters Seven and Eight relate some of the unique ways that God's Spirit inspired different people to respond, serve, and reach out (for example, the Friday lunches, "Watersports," the "New Wine" drama group, simplicity of lifestyle, the shack in the market place, the "Open to God" commitment campaign, prophecy, the "Saturday Shop," leadership in prayer, preaching, and organization). Can you identify gifts and abilities that various members of your congregation (including yourself!) could offer for the Holy Spirit to use in God's service? What are some of the ways in which you could encourage each other to develop these gifts and ministries?

Chapter 8

Gifts for the Body

One of the "Gifts for the Body" related in Chapter Eight is the following prophecy, addressed one Sunday morning to the congregation of St Nic's:

> **"You say you love one another and care for one another, but I know that in this congregation there is much loneliness and hurt that is not shared. You carry your needs, guilt and fear away, not realizing that you are a healing community. My children! I call upon you to love one another as brothers and sisters—to share in deeper ways than you have ever done; to be reckless in your love for me and others."**

Where are the "hidden" needs in your congregation, how can you become more of a healing community, and in what way might you be called to be "reckless in your love" for God and each other?

Chapter 9

Prison, Praise, and People

Chapter Nine, "Prison, Praise, and People," contains the following principles for developing and putting into practice a vision for spiritual growth:

__ Clarity of purpose from "the minister and at least some of the people"

__ "Divine discontent" with the present situation

__ An openness to new possibilities and change

__ Sharing and testing goals with other Christians

__ Deep, committed, and urgent prayer

__ Fasting

__ Having lay people make decisions for their own church

__ Dividing tasks among working committees

Which of these are already present in your congregation? Which can you help to bring about? Which are most important for your situation?

Chapter 10

Miracle at Easter

In Chapter Ten, "Miracle at Easter," Carey writes:

> **Who says that the Christian faith is a dull and miserable affair? We were learning that having fun and laughing together was not incompatible with following Christ. It even brought outsiders to him as well, who were attracted by joyful Christians.**

In what ways does your congregation make fun and laughter part of following Christ? Who are the most joyful Christians in your congregation, and in what ways can their enthusiasm help to make your church more attractive?

Chapter 11

Pull Us Out—It's Madness!

Chapters Ten and Eleven focus primarily on fundraising and the combination of excitement, controversy, and discouragement that accompanied the building project. As Carey describes it, initial "euphoria" gave way to "considerable heartsearching and hesitation." In fact, he says, "I came perilously close to pulling the plug on the whole thing." Through this difficult process, the people of St Nic's discovered the importance of trust in God's provision, the need for maintaining spiritual priorities, as well as for hard work and sacrificial giving, the danger of personal crises, and the power of Christian fellowship. Which of these lessons are most applicable to your personal situation, and that of your church?

Chapter 12

Exile

Chapter Twelve, "Exile," brings together stories of several new beginnings, some of them constructive and some divisive: charismatic renewal conferences, tearing up the old church building, worshiping in the Town Hall, the arrival of a new curate, the establishment of a house church, several baptisms, and a Christmas wedding in the half-renovated church. In your congregation, what has been the most constructive or unifying new initiative, what has been the most divisive, and in each case, why? What have you learned as a result about the process of change and the principles involved?

Chapter 13

Lessons of Faith

Among the "Lessons of Faith" recounted in Chapter Thirteen are the following:

- "We were learning that God could be trusted."
- "We were also learning the radical nature of faith" (that it involves significant risk and personal sacrifice).
- "We were also discovering God's resources in one another."
- "A third factor we were learning about was our own weakness."
- "We were also learning the lesson of being a fellowship of the Holy Spirit."

Which of these lessons of faith is most important for you, or for your congregation, at the present time? To what situations in particular do they apply?

Chapter 14

What—No Pews?

In Chapter Fourteen, a visitor to the newly renovated church compares St Nic's with the nearby cathedral, with the one a humbling reflection of God's majesty and the other symbolizing God's intimate love and acceptance. Carey takes this as "a reminder that no one church can possibly meet the needs of all people." Discuss with other members of your congregation how the architecture, worship style, and ministries of your church reflect particular aspects of God's character, and which of the needs around you your church is best able to meet.

Chapter 15

Facing the Future

For Carey, "Facing the Future" takes two forms. "First, Christians should live out their faith in their jobs and in the community . . . Second, the Church should take direct action in publicizing its life and message." In what ways does your own church already support community involvement and evangelism on the part of its members? If it was up to you, what further practical steps would you encourage your church to take toward the realization of these two goals? Specifically, what kind of assistance or support would help you to articulate and live out your faith outside the walls of your church?

CONCLUSION

Comparing your own situation to that which Carey describes in *The Church in the Market Place* will no doubt suggest a number of exciting possibilities, as well as posing some important challenges. The following questions will help you to think about the way forward for your own church.

- What role or responsibility do each of the following have in contributing to the growth of your church:
  - God (or more specifically, the Holy Spirit)?
  - Congregational leaders (clergy, vestry, parish council/advisory board)?
  - Parish organization, committee or group leaders and members?
  - Members of the congregation?
- What is the greatest asset, strength, or resource that will help your church to grow spiritually? The greatest liability or difficulty to be overcome?
- With God's help, what changes can your church accomplish immediately? in the next year? in the next five years?
- What can you contribute to the spiritual growth of your church, and in what way would you like your church to help you grow?

86905